WEST CHESTER PUBLIC LIB

P9-EMN-142

First Cookbooks

A Halloween
COOKBOOK

Simple Recipes for Kids

by Sarah L. Schuette

CAPSTONE PRESS
a capstone imprint

First Facts is published by Capstone Press,
1710 Roe Crest Drive, North Mankato, Minnesota 56003.
www.capstonepub.com

Copyright © 2012 by Capstone Press, a Capstone imprint.
All rights reserved.
No part of this publication may be reproduced in whole or in part, or stored in a
retrieval system, or transmitted in any form or by any means, electronic, mechanical, photocopying,
recording, or otherwise, without written permission of the publisher.
For information regarding permission, write to Capstone Press,
1710 Roe Crest Drive, North Mankato, Minnesota 56003.

Books published by Capstone Press are manufactured with paper
containing at least 10 percent post-consumer waste.

Library of Congress Cataloging-in-Publication Data
Schuette, Sarah L., 1976–
 A Halloween cookbook : simple recipes for kids / by Sarah L. Schuette.
  p. cm. — (First facts. First cookbooks)
 Includes bibliographical references and index.
 Summary: "Provides instructions and step-by-step photos for making a variety of simple snacks and
drinks with a Halloween theme"—Provided by publisher.
 ISBN 978-1-4296-7619-9 (library binding)
 1. Halloween cooking—Juvenile literature. 2. Cookbooks. I. Title. II. Series.

 TX739.2.H34S38 2012
 641.5'68—dc23   2011030287

Editorial Credits
Christine Peterson editor; Ashlee Suker, designer; Sarah Schuette, photo stylist; Marcy Morin, studio
     scheduler; Kathy McColley, production specialist

Photo Credits
All photos by Capstone Studio/Karon Dubke except:
Shutterstock: Alexander Potapov (spider web), 3, 4, Alhovik (spider), 4, javarman (grunge forest),
throughout, koya979 (gravestone), cover, 4 (bottom)

The author dedicates this book to Desmond G. Harper.

Printed in the United States of America in North Mankato, Minnesota.
102011
006405CGS12

Table of Contents

Frightening Foods

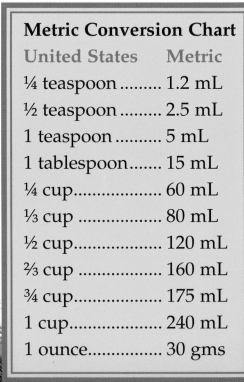

On Halloween things go bump in the night and in the kitchen. Time to whip up some ghoulishly good Halloween snacks. Hitch a broom ride into the kitchen and get started. Frightened of what's in the cupboards? There's no trick about it. Be brave, and take a look inside for your **ingredients**. Got questions? An adult can help.

Before you start, wash all of the slime and **cobwebs** from your hands. Be ghostlike and try not to make a mess. Don't forget to clean up your **cauldron** when you're through. After making these frightening foods, you'll be sure to have a happy Halloween!

Metric Conversion Chart	
United States	**Metric**
¼ teaspoon	1.2 mL
½ teaspoon	2.5 mL
1 teaspoon	5 mL
1 tablespoon	15 mL
¼ cup	60 mL
⅓ cup	80 mL
½ cup	120 mL
⅔ cup	160 mL
¾ cup	175 mL
1 cup	240 mL
1 ounce	30 gms

Tools

Ghosts rattle chains. Witches wave wands.
The right equipment makes for a scary good time.
Use this handy guide to gather the tools you'll need.

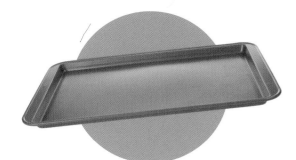

baking sheet—a flat, metal pan used for baking foods

cutting board—a wooden or plastic board used when slicing or chopping foods

dry-ingredient measuring cups—round cups with handles used for measuring dry ingredients

liquid measuring cup—a glass or plastic measuring cup with a spout for pouring

measuring spoons—spoons with small deep scoops used to measure both wet and dry ingredients

microwave-safe bowl—a non-metal bowl used to heat ingredients in a microwave oven

pitcher—a container with an open top and a handle that is used to hold liquids

pot holders—a thick, heavy fabric that is used to handle hot items

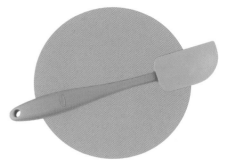

rubber scraper—a kitchen tool with a rubber paddle on one end

skewer—a long, thin stick used to hold food

strainer—a bowl-shaped tool with holes in the sides and bottom used for draining liquid off food

wooden spoon—a tool made of wood with a handle used to mix ingredients

Techniques

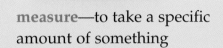

measure—to take a specific amount of something

slice—to cut into thin pieces

spread—to cover a surface with something

sprinkle—to scatter in small drops or bits

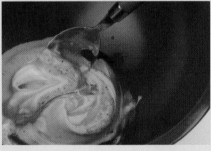

stir—to mix something by moving a spoon around in it

toss—to mix gently with two spoons or forks

Jack-o'-Lantern Juice

Don't like scooping out the guts but love that pumpkin taste? Then give this tasty drink a try. It will put a smile on your jack-o'-lantern.

Serves 2

Ingredients:
- ½ cup canned pumpkin
- 2 cups orange juice
- ¼ teaspoon ground ginger
- fat-free whipped topping
- dash of cinnamon

Tools:
- dry-ingredient measuring cups
- pitcher
- liquid measuring cup
- measuring spoons
- wooden spoon
- glass

TIP:
Dip a graham cracker in your juice, and it will taste like pumpkin pie!

1 Measure and add pumpkin to a pitcher.

2 Measure and add orange juice to pitcher.

3 Measure ginger and add to pumpkin mixture and stir.

4 Pour juice into glass.

5 Add whipped topping to **garnish**. Sprinkle cinnamon on top.

Crunchy Spiders

Spiders have eight legs to quickly catch **prey** in their webs. Turn the tables on these crunchy spiders. Gobble them up as quickly as you can.

Serves 2

Ingredients:
- 4 round vanilla or chocolate cookies
- 2 tablespoons peanut butter
- 16 thin pretzel sticks
- white chocolate chips

Tools:
- plate
- spoon
- measuring spoons

TIP:
You can also use crackers and spreadable cheese for this treat.

1 Place two cookies on a plate.

2 Using a spoon, spread 1 tablespoon of peanut butter on each of the cookies.

3 Place remaining cookies on top of peanut butter.

4 Press pretzel sticks into the peanut butter to make eight legs.

5 Place two small drops of peanut butter on top of each cookie sandwich.

6 Place white chocolate chips on the peanut butter to make eyes.

11

Slithery Sandwiches

Hungry for a scaly snack? **Slither** on up to the table, and sink your teeth into these snakelike sandwiches. You'll have energy to trick or treat all night long.

Serves 1

Ingredients:
- shredded lettuce
- 2 breadsticks with flat bottoms
- 2 tablespoons fat-free cream cheese
- 2 slices American cheese
- 2 slices deli meat
- 2 black olive slices
- 1 red pepper strip

Tools:
- plate
- spoon
- knife

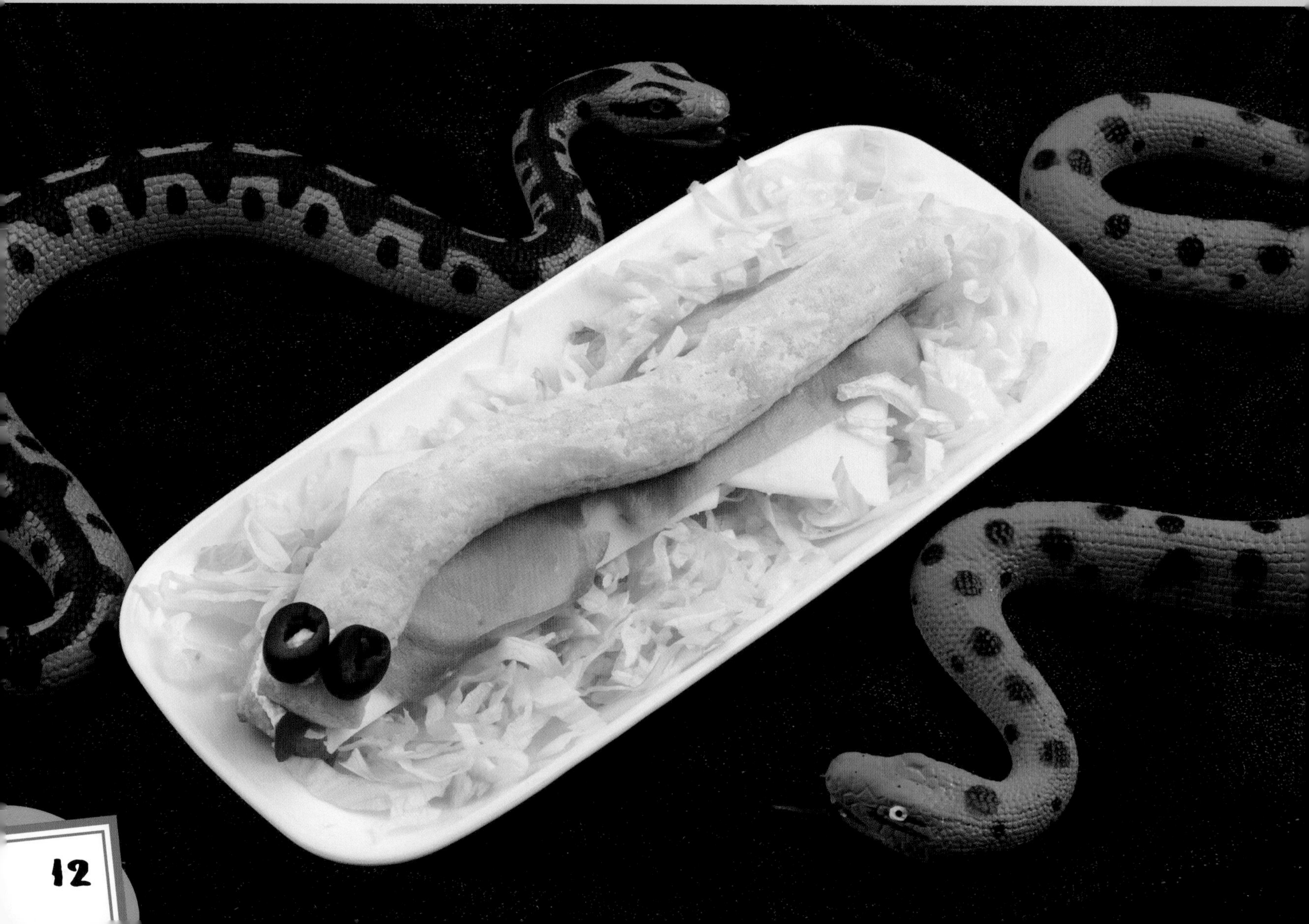

 1 Sprinkle shredded lettuce on a plate.

2 Lay one breadstick on the plate.

3 Spread cream cheese on the breadstick with a spoon.

4 Add cheese slices and meat to breadstick. Top with the other breadstick slice.

5 Using a little cream cheese like glue, add the olives to look like eyes.

6 Have an adult cut the red pepper to look like a tongue. Add to sandwich.

Monster Toes

Monsters don't usually wear shoes. Instead they stomp through forests with their bare, stinky feet. Lucky for you, these monster toes are much cleaner. And their smell will make your mouth water.

Serves 2

Ingredients:

- ½ cup fat-free mayonnaise
- 1 tablespoon yellow mustard
- 1 tablespoon Dijon mustard
- 2 tablespoons honey
- ½ teaspoon lemon juice
- 1 8-ounce bag of fresh sugar snap peas

Tools:

- small mixing bowl
- dry-ingredient measuring cups
- measuring spoons
- spoon
- plate
- small serving bowl

TIP:
Ask an adult to cut the pea pods open. Then stuff the insides of the pods with dressing!

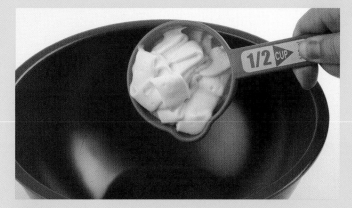

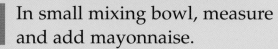

1 In small mixing bowl, measure and add mayonnaise.

2 Measure and add yellow mustard and Dijon mustard.

3 Measure honey and lemon juice, and add to bowl. Stir with spoon.

4 Arrange snap peas around the serving bowl.

5 Pour dip into serving bowl. Dunk your monster toes into the dip and enjoy!

15

Eyeball Salad

Who knew eyeballs could make such a tasty salad?
The trick is using round vegetables instead of actual eyeballs.
See how this salad fills you up—all the way to your eyeballs.

Serves 2

Ingredients:

- ¾ cup basil **pesto**
- 1 tablespoon olive oil
- 1 cup pre-cooked pasta
- 1 cup sliced black olives
- 1 cup cherry tomatoes
- 2 sticks string cheese

Tools:

- large mixing bowl
- measuring spoons
- 2 spoons
- dry-ingredient measuring cups
- butter knife
- cutting board

1 In a large mixing bowl, measure and add pesto and olive oil. Mix well.

2 Add the pasta to the bowl. Toss to coat.

3 Next add the black olives and cherry tomatoes. Stir.

4 With an adult's help, slice the string cheese into small, round, pieces on a cutting board.

5 Add cheese slices to salad and stir.

TIP:
Try making an eyeball fruit salad with grapes, blueberries, and other round fruits. No need for a sauce, just mix together and enjoy.

Witch Fingernails

Witches cast spells with their bony fingers that have long, pointed nails. These crunchy fingernails are sure to cast a spell on your friends.

Serves 2

Ingredients:
- 1 cup pumpkin seeds
- 1 teaspoon olive oil
- 1 teaspoon seasoning salt

Tools:
- dry-ingredient measuring cups
- small mixing bowl
- measuring spoons
- spoon
- microwave-safe plate

 1 Measure pumpkin seeds, and add to bowl.

2 Measure and pour oil over seeds. Stir seeds with a spoon until coated in oil.

3 Pour seeds onto plate. Microwave seeds for five to eight minutes.

4 With an adult's help, stir the warm seeds once each minute. The fingernails are done when they turn brown and are crispy.

 5 Sprinkle pumpkin seeds with seasoning salt, and stir to coat evenly. Let cool.

TIP:
Mix in some wasabi peas to look like warts!

19

Freaked-Out Fruit

Put these freaked-out fruits out of their pain.
Wolf them down before they disappear into someone
else's stomach.

Serves 4

Ingredients:

- 2 large marshmallows
- 2 to 4 strawberries
- 2 to 4 blackberries
- 1 cup chocolate chips
- 1 cup white chocolate chips
- 1 large grapefruit
- black and white gel icing tubes

Tools:

- skewers
- dry-ingredient measuring cups
- microwave-safe bowls
- spoon
- baking sheet
- parchment paper
- knife
- cutting board
- plate

TIP:
Want black and white fruit? After dipping in one color, use a fork to drizzle the other color on top for a fancier look.

1 Push one skewer into each marshmallow, strawberry, and blackberry.

2 Measure and pour chocolate chips into two microwave-safe bowls. Heat for one minute and stir.

3 Hold skewers and dip each into melted chocolate.

4 Set fruit and marshmallows on baking sheet with parchment paper to harden for 30 minutes.

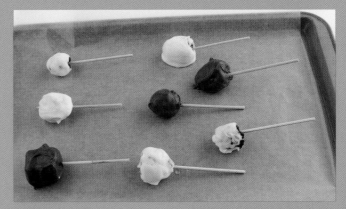

5 While you wait, have an adult cut the grapefruit in half on a cutting board. Place cut side down on plate.

6 Use icing to give your fruit scary faces. Stick the skewers into the grapefruit.

21

Glossary

cauldron (KOL-dren)—a large kettle, often associated with witches' brew

cobweb (KOB-web)—a very fine net of sticky threads made by a spider to catch flies and other insects

garnish (GAR-nish)—to decorate food with small amounts of other foods or spices

ingredient (in-GREE-dee-uhnt)—an item used to make something else

pesto (PES-toh)—a sauce made from basil, nuts, oil, and cheese that is usually served with pasta

prey (PRAY)—an animal that is hunted by another animal for food

slither (SLITH-ur)—to slide along like a snake

Read More

Llewellyn, Claire. *Cooking with Fruits and Vegetables.* Cooking Healthy. New York: Rosen Central, 2012.

Malam, John. *Grow Your Own Snack.* Grow It Yourself! Chicago: Heinemann Library, 2012.

Schuette, Sarah L. *A Monster Cookbook: Simple Recipes for Kids.* First Cookbooks. Mankato, Minn.: Capstone Press, 2011.

Internet Sites

FactHound offers a safe, fun way to find Internet sites related to this book. All of the sites on FactHound have been researched by our staff.

Here's all you do:

Visit *www.facthound.com*

Type in this code: 9781429676199

Super-cool stuff!

Check out projects, games and lots more at
www.capstonekids.com

Index